This Will Pass

∽

Poems

by

Ed Krizek

This Will Pass: Poems

© Ed Krizek 2021

ISBN: 978-1-941066-47-8

Book design by Jo-Anne Rosen

Wordrunner Press
Petaluma, California

For Caroline,

Always

Acknowledgements

Some of the poems in this volume were previously published as follows:

"Hope," *The Non-Conformist*, July 2020

"Pandemic," *North of Oxford*, Spring 2020

"Path to Wellness," *The Buddhist Poetry Review*, Spring 2020

"Night Sky," *Broadkill Review*, Jan/Feb 2020

"Sunset Beach," *The Swarthmorean*, April 5, 2019

"Honesty," *The Swarthmorean*, April 5, 2019

"Evening At Home," *The Swarthmorean*, April 5, 2019

"Early Spring," *The Swarthmorean*, April 5, 2019

"Rorschach," *Art Through the Eyes of Mad Poets*, April 2019

"Lakeside," *Slab*, April 2019

"The Craftsman," *Slab*, April 2019

"Some Poems," *Poetry Ink*, April 2018

"Haikus," *Mad Poets Review*, 2002

Contents

This Will Pass

This Light Will Fade

The sweetness of raisins in milk
lingers on my tongue.
A thought drifts
as a breeze shifts
on the sunlit surface
of the ocean.

Still, this light will fade
as will the raisin's sugary taste.

Achilles wished to be remembered.
I have wished the same.
But I know this will not happen.
And truly it doesn't matter
because
I have held a raisin in my mouth,
seen the glint of the sun on the ocean,
and heard wave after wave connect
with the shore. Their sound floats
up to the sky
flying away
with the birds.

Night Sky

After The Hidden Moon by Birge Harrison 1907

Moon hiding behind   night clouds.
Faint hearted
I stare at the painting.

The night is stark   and black.
   like the mysteries   of the subconscious.

As I gaze   into the night sky
   moonlight diffuses around the clouds of paint
which seems to move
with an unseen   wind.

Moonlight is   but a reflection   of our star
   just as conscious patter   derives   from the subconscious.

On the precipice   of speech   words emerge
out of the swirling —

self, poised
to be revealed

When You Are Seventy

For Georgia

No wise man ever wished to be young again.
— Jonathan Swift

If you are seventy today,
you are old enough
to have seen a man
land on the moon —
old enough to have seen
Nixon resign —
old enough to have seen
our first Black president elected.

You are old enough
to claim a discount at the theater,
and have the other patrons
invite you to the head
of the line.
You can fall asleep
at parties without
anyone thinking
less of you.
When you misbehave,
you are old enough
to know better.

When you are seventy
you are young enough

to laugh with a child —
young enough to marvel
at the rebirth of spring —
young enough to care.

You are able to look
backwards and forwards
with wistful wisdom
and realize that life,
your life
is a gift.

This Will Pass

In the height of summer
life erupts in glorious
green leaves, flying birds,
chirping insects.

This will pass.

I mourn the loss
of summer as leaves turn red
and fall.
On cloudy days
I have searched desperately
for the sun.

Success is like this;
it comes and goes like summer.
We mourn its loss
and seek it
among fallen dreams.

This will pass.

We are taught
to desire success
perhaps fame.
We do not question
but believe in their permanence.

This will pass.

Failure is as sure as success
though we are taught to fear it
not mention it
speak only of joy.

As surely as success
failure passes.

We know nothing of the future.
We long for the stable and permanent
reaching for hand holds
among the rocks and roots.
We are part of this
as long as our heart beats.

This will pass.

We hold our future
and our end together for a time.
We honor our gift
when we accept both
without celebration
without regret.

Rorschach

After "Little Painting with Yellow (Improvisations)
   by Vasily Kandinsky

Planets and galaxies linger
in static tension
like celestial dancers
as hot yellow burns.
Chaotic confluence of color
leaps and soars
in the patois of abstraction.
Perhaps our swirling
cosmic rainbow
will yield
understanding.

Our unconscious dance continues
as we exist, sometimes cautiously
measuring our days,
sometimes cavorting
like vibrant devas
freely performing
alien gambols
unencumbered by propriety
or convention.

Jordan's Room

Sun streams
in white curtains.
From a skylight I can see
evergreens and elms swaying
as they try to touch the floating clouds.

Today has been a lazy day. I rose,
ate, napped, ate again,
and listened to jazz all afternoon.
Not the avant-garde jazz of Ornette Coleman,
but the straight-ahead forms of Ahmad Jamal
and Oscar Peterson. There is comfort
in the riffs and melodies spoken
by my tiny speakers. It is
a private conversation between me
and the music. As the dialogue continues
I see butterflies, ferns, and winged fairies.
The painted bees go about their business.
As my mind drifts
to the edges of unreal beliefs.
My adult fear is eased by a child's whimsy,
the kind that elevates the ordinary to the sacred.

Haikus

Beauty

The heart of the pearl
holds a single silica
grain of ill feeling.

Insight

A small spark lights up
our dark rooms. For a moment
we see the cobwebs.

Desire

We grasp the stream's wet
only to find dry air drops
between our fingers.

Less Travelled

I have sometimes taken that road
by necessity, not choice.
There the jungle thrives.
There insects and serpents threaten.
Spanish moss alive with chiggers.
Fallen leaves crawl
as I tentatively move forward.
In the darkness
shivering
I strike a light
which burns my hands,
shows the way.

Yellow Roses

Such a long, long time to be gone
and a short time to be there.
  — *Robert Hunter*

With time the sadness passes.
Occasionally, though, a memory pokes up
organically as if from the soil itself.
Died and cremated fifteen years ago,
my emotions have had time to
germinate, age, mature.

It's not the photo on the shelf
that prompts the return of sadness
that brings me to tears.
What else is there to do
isolated in quarantine
waiting for life to begin again.

My loss blooms
into a bouquet
of yellow roses trimmed in crimson,
the kind my father used to give her
when she had a minor car accident or
made a foolish mistake.
On Google it says they can mean love
or farewell.

Soon it will be June when all the roses
will blossom. Time will have sealed the hole
in my gut. But for now, I remember her
and think of yellow roses.

Sunset Beach

1.
Clouds cover the sky
offering a gray fluorescence.
Cormorants dive for fish
from the remnants
of an old wreck.
Rusted and unrecognizable
the mangled metal provides
the basis for a food chain
that ends with these black birds.
It is peculiar, I think,
that the wind blows
so cold from the sea
and all the Cape May diamonds
have been collected by tourists
leaving only broken shells
and the occasional cigarette butt.

2.
There is only one poem.
I have written it many times.
It's the one where I discuss
the miracle of life,
marvel at precious human existence
then wonder why death
always gets the upper hand.
Love is the one steady light

in the darkness of the universe
breaking through all barriers
and adding eternal energy to our dust.

3.
The sun is now a hazy white disk
hovering around two o'clock
in the rainy sky. The row
of white Adirondack chairs
facing the ocean calls out for visitors
None come, save my wife and me.
We sit, watch the swells on the ocean,
white caps in the wind like
the calm we feel. On a pole
an American flag pops
and flaps in the breeze.

Smoke

I thought of you again
today, after many years,
and I became a poem.
I became a letter
and a book. I mailed
myself to your office
in a package marked
Personal.

The poem went on about
how I am doing and my recent life.
It was poignant
about the memories we share
but a bit grasping.

The letter tried to explain the poem.
It was really not good at doing that.
The book was a gift, an anthology
of poems called *Healing the Divide.*
I ordered a copy from Amazon.

Then I went to lie with my wife.
I rubbed her naked back,
and remembered all the past packages
sent to you with no response.

We are older now.
The letter entreated you for some
acknowledgement of who we were
forty years ago when you said,
I want to have your children.

After rubbing my wife's back for five minutes
I got up, cancelled the book order.

This is the poem.

The letter drifted away
like the smoke of a passing flame.

Pandemic

Today I took myself out
of quarantine. The sun
was welcoming,
the temperature mild,
sky blue and almost cloudless.

We are walking
on charnel ground,
trying to avoid death
by embracing life,
from six feet away,

Reality is the present
as the virus multiplies.
I am not afraid of death,

just not ready.

New Hampshire Lakeside

(Lake Winnepessaukee)

1.
It is not that there is nothing
to say. Laughing skies
and sailboats cry out
for explanation.
Interior exploration leads
to molten moments of consciousness
reawakening like daffodils in spring.
Life requires attention!
Looking in the mirror
or out the window,
face lined with furrows
of confusion, I ask
the wind for an answer.
The gray water laps the shore.

2.
As I age memories rise
from pools of the past.
The taste of sugar and milk
in coffee reminds me
of a sunlit Sunday in Menlo Park, CA
before I lost my mind.
I read The New York Times
and drank cup after cup
of sweet coffee. Today
I take my coffee without additives.
Perhaps not as sweet but real.

4.
Small ships cross
the horizon or disappear
behind an island. I hear
laughter in the wind.

5.
The waitress in the red shirt
and tan shorts says it's all right
to take up a table for an hour
while I wait for my wife.
The Dockside Restaurant doesn't seem
busy. Everyone mentions the weather.
Nice day! Beautiful day!
I write in a notebook and hope.

The Craftsman

For Adam

Mottled marble
cracked and multi-colored
shows layers of time
made smooth
by the craftsman's hands.

Working in obscurity
he shapes and polishes
simple rock
which matures into art.

The masses marvel.

Seeing only the beauty
of his creation
they stand
with dropped jaws
and eyes agape
then turn
and walk away,
muttering.

The craftsman is oblivious.
He continues working,
communing with the task
he has chosen,
attention absorbed

by every crevasse
in this stone
which he has consecrated
with his struggle.

Hospice

An old woman
is dying,
like many
old women, old men.

An old woman
is dying
in an old peoples' home,
a facility with cinder block walls
painted a neutral shade
and artificial light that seems
very cold.

An old woman
is dying,
Childless,
she thinks
of those she loved,
those who loved her,
those she is leaving.

An old woman
is dying.
that I know through
a friend. She corrected my etiquette,
suggested I become
passionate about losing weight.

Just an old woman
dying,
and the fact that old people
are dying
makes little difference
to the living world.

But I just heard.
My morning coffee
has become cold,
and my desire to go on
has stopped,
as I stare straight ahead
wet-faced,
at nothing in particular.

In Autumn

Once long ago I went apple picking
with a woman I loved. The day
was cool but not cold and overcast.
Together we picked a bushel of apples.
It took six paper grocery bags
to bring them away with us.
As we left the haze lifted.
You could see the sun set.

She lived at home with her parents.
so I carried the apples to my apartment.
I made apple pie, apple brown betty,
apple strudel, apple cake, baked apples,
applesauce. We both agreed
these treats were delicious.

I couldn't use all the apples.
Eventually a few went bad.
Then more. Finally,
I had to throw what remained
down the chute that went
to nowhere I had ever seen.

We broke up because she wanted
a man who could support a family.
All I could do was cook.

She married a guy named George
I think he was some kind of engineer.

I haven't been apple picking since then.
But my wife wants to go next weekend.
I think I'll join her!

Honesty

In the dark night
I can feel your body
and touch places
we do not name.
Useless eyes close
I dream of the unmentionable
lover who arrives
when we sleep.
My restlessness heightens
as quiet starlight
illuminates an angelic face.
Embracing duplicity
I am whole again.
My lover flees
in the light of day
leaving a void
that drinks my spirit
drains my blood
moves me forward.

Greetings from Florida

Day 1.

The hotel's coffee maker broke.
I'm looking forward to brewing
the new machine's first pot of coffee.
I dedicate this cup to you, Florida
and as I sip,
like Aesop's fox,
I say to myself,
I never liked you that much, anyway.

Wish you were here
and I was there.

Day 2.

Today is Tax Day.
Today we tell the government
how much we owe it,
or how much it owes us.
Sitting in an alley café in Tarpon Springs, Florida
Judge Judy is talking on the television
that hangs above a gathering of white tables.

Something about the way the light shines
through the skylight on the second-floor balcony
reminds me of Astoria, Queens.
Maybe it's just the Greeks.
They came to dive for sponges in the Gulf.

Could also be the sign in the upstairs window that reads:
HOME LOANS.

The girl behind the counter
says she's done with men.
Done with men and she can't be
more than twenty-five.

I am under the illusion
that I am happy sitting at a table
in an alley café.

Day 3.

Watch the sun set into the Gulf —
A group of odd-looking strangers approaches
asks me where I'm from.

Philadelphia.

A hand extends in my direction.
I take it.
Nothing bad happens.

Back in the suite
with the door double locked
I am afraid.
I am fat.
Not tough anymore.
None of my friends are tough anymore.

Day 4.

I dreamed that I saw my lost friends
my lost cousin, my lost family.
All the places and people I've lost
come back to me
and I remember why I loved them,
remember why they loved me.

Day 5.

Fort Desoto County Park.
Sit in the sun.
Not enough time for a tan.

Birds and fish.
We are all eating each other
Gary Snyder says.
Florida looked like this
before all the paved roads and condos
erupted on the dunes.

Day 6.

I drink twenty-one-year-old single malt
become maudlin about my lost youth.

Day 7.

But I watched the sun set with Caroline tonight.
Afterwards the moon rose in the east.

Snapshots

May your life be interesting,
says a Chinese curse.

And so, it has been.

Seeing snapshots, I found
inside a file cabinet's bottom drawer

I found some of the forgotten love
from years ago. Unmistakable.

Felt the longing for the past
intensely. Baby pictures, high school, college.

Cards to my mother she saved. Letters
from her dripping with love

like mourning tears,
that have dried but are not gone.

Those easy laughing times
yielding up unimaginable

empty spaces
to fill.

Hope

Happy to see
the sun again,
I dance
in the morning air
screaming out
that life is good.
Only the gulls
hear me.
Despair's seductive song
calls to me
yet I hear
another voice.
She silences
this empty enchantress.
Her promise
sends me running
headlong
into the day.

Evening at Home

She is constant like the ocean.
Gentle currents carry her warmth.
I sit waiting.
It is night.
A quarter moon lights my balcony.
The fire burns.
I wait
knowing she will appear
before the light has gone,
the fire out.
Patiently I sip my tea
wondering
how all this came to be
when I know
it could have been otherwise.
Baffled by my good fortune
distraught over what might have been
her key turns in our front door
while the moon is hidden
by a nighttime cloud
and the fire burns
bright.

Dolphin

Blue against blue
he bursts the water
flying in air,
his streamlined body
a projectile hurdling
toward an unknown galaxy.
To break free
his body shapes
into a perfect arc
gaining speed.
Not fish, not of land
he has no wish
to be limited
yet, has no choice
but to be a prisoner
constrained
by natural law
and the conditions
of his birth.

Winter Solstice

*The moment the darkness is greatest is when the
light return*
— Robin Wall Kemmerer

In the darkness
of winter's womb
I rest and reflect
alone.

You are born alone
and die alone
my mother used to say.

I think of her now
turned to ash.

Deep in winter's night
cocooned in memories
I lie in fetal position
amidst warm bedclothes.

I watch joy
and longing
pass through
my mind.

The darkness comforts
my solitude.
The dark not of gloom
but of hope.
I wait for the light
knowing it will come.

Early Spring

Wind blows the water's surface
sending a small chill.
A single mallard dives.
Cyclists and walkers patrol
her circumference. Some
bring their dogs for a jolt
of sun and fair skies.
Man-made Lake Galena
has become a natural wonder.
There's something calming
about the water.
Still early spring, I gaze
across her surface marveling
at rippling caused by a steady
northeast wind. My mind freezes
the moment in a memory that presses
my thoughts. No photo can capture
the gentle ease of a white gull
landing with a splash.

A Wreath for Eddie

I was named "Edwin"
after my father.
My mother called him "Eddie."
He was young
when he died at forty-four.
For thirty-five years
until her death
my mother paid
a local florist
to place a wreath
on his grave at Christmas.

Neither she nor I
visited the grave much.
When we did
we could see
these decaying remnants
of remembrance.

I hadn't been to
my father's grave for years
when my mother passed.
When I found the florist's bill
I called the number
told them to stop.

Now it is Christmas again.
I seek out relatives

and old friends
trying to find our connection.
Still I feel something's awry.

My mother is not in the plot with my father.
She wanted her ashes scattered
in Glacier National Park.
He is two thousand miles away
in New York City.
But can see his marble monument
as I smoke cigarettes
at night on my balcony
in twenty-degree Pennsylvania weather.
I look up at the stars
and consider our planet's smallness
my own existence.
I want to touch something
I'm not sure is there.
I think of the unspoiled snow
in Glacier that comforts my Mom.
I remember Eddie,
the man she loved.
In the morning I call the cemetery
and have a wreath placed
at the foot of his
rose-colored stone.

Path to Wellness

1.
Suburban Jungle

In an upscale section
of the suburbs, this afternoon,
this coffee shop
has only female customers.

They all wear well-coordinated
outfits of gray, black, and white.
The room sounds as if filled
with birds, howler monkeys,
and other jungle animals.

Someone is playing rap.
Ferns, Ivy and bamboo
cover one inside wall.
The women come and go.

2.
Zen Garden

I am ailing hoping for health.
My sickness is a bit better.
Coughing less.
Should not have smoked last week.
(Note to self: Don't Smoke!)
My chest would hurt less
if I hadn't run my car into that truck.

The solemnity of the garden
brings calm contentment.
as I wander through the woods
with no particular path.

Flute in distance calls
forward, forward. Thoughts
drift past and disappear.
What is the Buddha?

All we have is what we experience.
Embrace now, pain as well as pleasure.

3.
Dukkha

Pain and suffering can be transient
more or less. The mind
experiences the effects
of pain and illness.
They are real
But not our true selves.

There is beauty
in the smell of manure
as it wafts across the fields
signaling life continues.
Amish farms powered by horses
populate the countryside.
Washed clothes hang on lines outside.

4.

Meditation

Life is sleeping.
On the highway,
Semis growl along
in both directions.
Their onerous rumble
jolts. Yet it is possible
to find calm inside
the space in your head.
It can be tended, nurtured
and made to fit you own
vision.

5.

Presence

I have lived
and thrived
in a variety of US subcultures.
The past is past.
The future has not yet happened.
I am lost in a dream.
My wife is snoring
as I write stream of consciousness
into a small notebook.
The riffs of language matter
only to me. They resound
off the walls of my mind,
bells pealing joy.

Untitled

The purest emotion
is the wind blowing
dandelion down
across a freshly mowed lawn.

Some Poems

are erudite like a college professor
at a colloquium discussing
aspects of post-modernism in art
over Courvoisier and black caviar.
These verses can be so obtuse the mind strains
in its straight-jacket of anguished rumbling
grasping at their meaning
as they flow silently into obscurity.

Some poems are difficult to understand
at first reading requiring further study.
One turns phrases and images over
on a spit above a mental roasting fire
gently basting each word with tenderness
while drops of emotion rendered
by the heat drip
into the coals and turn to smoke.

Some poems are straightforward,
truthful, but not, necessarily, simple.
They can be understood with a clear mind
not requiring the reader to drink herself
into a flaccid jellyfish to evoke
awareness, or to pry open its structure
like a hungry starfish with an oyster
before offering up a pearl